INTERNET MARKETING TIPS FOR BUSY EXECUTIVES

Simple Ways to Improve Your Internet Presence

Peter Alexander & John Nobrega

Writers Club Press
San Jose New York Lincoln Shanghai

Internet Marketing Tips for Busy Executives
Simple Ways to Improve Your Internet Presence

Published by Writers Club Press
an imprint of iUniverse.com, Inc.

For information address:
iUniverse.com, Inc.
620 North 48th Street
Suite 201
Lincoln, NE 68504-3467
www.iuniverse.com

ISBN: 0-595-10019-8

Printed in the United States of America

What Others Are Saying about Internet Marketing Tips for Busy Executives

"This is a classic case of "less is more". This little book is deceptive. It packs more real knowledge and usable ideas and tips into fewer pages than anything else on the market. The authors clearly have "been there—done that" when it comes to designing and supporting Web business."

Robert Frank
CEO, Open Commerce, Inc.
Pleasanton, California

"After spending $50+ on magazines and other books on how to successfully market my service via the Web, I wish I would have discovered this book initially. Why read a manual when the essential checklist has already been developed? This book includes hints and reminders helpful at the design stage all the way to site maintenance. Although marketed for executives, anyone who has an Internet presence will find the information in this book valuable. It's a resource that I'll use frequently."

Linda Aden
Educational Consultant
Lincoln, Nebraska

Acknowledgement

Bob Roloson of Rolo Graphics – *Artwork*.

This book is dedicated to all of our clients who have trusted our expertise in helping them improve their Internet presence.

Contents

WHY THIS BOOK?

A minority of the businesses in the United States has an Internet presence, and fewer than half of these companies are seeing a significant return on their Internet Marketing efforts. Why? Because these businesses don't know how to market their sites effectively to their target audience. They either take the "If you build it, they will come" approach or they expect their Web site developers to do the marketing for them. Unfortunately, most developers are graphic artists, not marketing specialists.

The tips included in this book are intended to give those with minimal knowledge of Internet Marketing techniques a simple way to develop an active, effective Web site. Anyone from a small business owner to a senior marketing executive within a large, global organization can use this book to quickly and easily make their company Web site better.

We recognize that time is a precious commodity and busy people do not have time to read a 300-page book. Therefore, each tip has purposely been made brief so you can get right to the point and spark ideas that will help make your Web sites more effective.

After reading the tips, you will be better prepared to discuss marketing needs with your Web site vendor and receive more value from your Internet marketing budget.

PLAN AHEAD

Plan: a method for achieving an end; a detailed formulation of a program of action; an orderly arrangement of parts of an overall design or objective.

How often are we in such a rush to get things done that we ignore the planning stage that would save us time, energy, and resources down the road? When it comes to effective Internet marketing, it's important that you don't succumb to the "I'll know it when I see it" mentality. Even if you implement only one of the planning tips below, you will be ahead of the game.

1.   Know why you're creating a Web site (goals and purpose). Sketch out a blueprint BEFORE you develop it.

2.   Determine the needs of your different customer groups and plan a design that caters to your most profitable customers. As much as 80 percent of your business can come from only 20 percent of your customers. Plan to deliver more value to that 20 percent than they expect.

3.   Most sites ignore one or two of the key audiences (customers, prospective employees, or shareholders) in favor of just one. Remember to keep a big picture perspective, and don't leave any key target audiences out.

4.   Develop a formal Internet Marketing Plan that you use as a working document. Update it on a quarterly basis to take advantage of market trends and technological advances.

5.   Branding on the Web requires an integrated marketing approach. In addition to Internet advertising and links, successful Web branding also requires a balanced communication mix using traditional media (TV, radio, print), direct marketing, sales promotion and, if appropriate, personal selling. The company must also sell a compelling product or service to get people talking, taking advantage of the most powerful form of advertising: word-of-mouth.

6. Advancing from a rudimentary site to one with modest features and goals requires buy-in from senior management and is a political process as much as a technical one. Educate the senior officers who don't believe the Internet is all that important.

7. Determine who in your organization will be responsible for the Web site. This is typically a time-consuming job, so make sure you budget adequate resources to handle the task. Don't just add it as an additional responsibility for someone in your company. This person won't have enough time in the day to handle other duties.

8. Once the site is built, how will you let people know it exists? Take a look at the Tactical, Advertising, Search Engine, and Community sections in this book. Then develop a plan to accomplish the strategies you choose at the same time your Web site is being developed.

9. Opening a merchant account with a bank to accept credit cards on your site can take several days, and registering your company with a credit card processing software company can take anywhere from one to

two weeks. To be safe, allow three to four weeks for all the registrations and paper-work for credit card transaction authoriza-tion to be finalized.

10. Although you're in the planning phase, don't procrastinate. Recognize that the longer you wait, the more difficult the task is likely to become and the more competitors will get ahead of you.

11. For each page you plan for your Web site, you should answer the following key questions:

◆"What do I want my visitors to know here?"
◆"What do I want my visitors to do at this point?"
◆"What do I want my visitors to feel right now?"
◆And, "Where do I want my visitors to go next?"

By answering these questions in the planning phase, your visitors will not be confused regarding the value of each page on your site.

DEVELOPMENT HINTS

Develop: to move from the original position to one providing more opportunity for effective use; to go through a process of natural growth, differentiation, or evolution by successive changes.

Once your plan is ready, the next step is to start the development phase of the project. This can be extremely challenging for non-technical marketing and business managers who are novices to Web site development because they must interface and communicate effectively with Web site developers who seem to be speaking another language.

Nonetheless, the development phase of the project will go more smoothly if you heed the following suggestions.

12. KISS (Keep It Simple Stupid). We're sure you have heard this phrase in the past, but we repeat it here because of its relevance. If you don't keep the site simple and consistent, your visitors will be confused and your Webmaster will be frustrated. When in doubt, less is better.

13. Secure a good domain name as soon as possible. It's like real estate on the Web and it caters to the first come, first served system. A

catchy domain name could be the difference between getting new visitors or losing them to another site with a more appealing domain name. It also makes it easier to remember for your visitors, clients, and prospects.

14. Other tips for choosing a unique and memorable domain include:

◈The "the" word: Try adding the word "the" before object names. For example, ThePostOffice.com as opposed to PostOffice.com.

◈Buzzwords: Place "e-words" such as "wired" before the required name, or perhaps "online" or "hotel" after it.

◈Alliterate: Using two words beginning with the same letter aids the memory—WinWinWeb.com is easier to remember than ChristmasInNew-England.com.

◈The shorter, the better: Never overestimate the memory span of the average Internet surfer – EveryNameOfYour-Company.co.uk is not a good choice.

◈Swap and change: If www.WinWin-Web.com wasn't available, we could have tried WebWinWin.com.

◈"Dot Com" it: always go for the .com option before trying .net, .org, or country-specific domains. People are used to .com, not the other extensions.

◈If a name you want is already taken, you might want to check to see if it is available for purchase. You can use the

"who is" search function at www.net-
worksolutions.com to determine the
registered owner of any .com, .net, or .org
domain name. To see lists of names
available for purchase, try a name auction
site such as www.greatdomains.com

15. Have complete contact information on your
site and make it easy for a visitor to find. It's
amazing how many sites forget to do this.
Include your phone number(s), fax number,
address and e-mail contact address. You
want to give your prospects every opportunity to contact you. And make sure that as
area codes or addresses change, they are
immediately updated on your site.

16. Avoid frames (a way of programming Web
pages) where possible. A large percentage of
your visitors will find you through search
engines and programming with frames hin-
ders most search engines from properly
indexing your site. Frame pages can be difficult for visitors to bookmark as well.

17. Avoid "under construction" signs. It looks
unprofessional. Just let visitors know when

the site will be updated and you can add the content when you're ready.

18. Don't have any missing pages or broken links in your site. Few things are more frustrating to a visitor then getting an error message (or nothing at all) when clicking on a link in your site. Site testing software and services are available to automate site testing for errors. One of the most popular resources is http://websitegarage.netscape.com.

19. Make sure your site is interesting and compelling. Even if your content is dry, there are

ways to be creative and add spice (see the Tactical Tips section).

20. Intuitive navigation is very important, because you don't want your visitors to get lost on your site. Create a global table of contents (starting with your home page) and have major sections of the table of contents available on each page so that visitors can easily click to whichever section of your site they are interested in.

21. Make sure to supply text labels for each navigational button for better search engine reception and for visitors with text-only browsers.

22. Look at your site with a text only browser (such as Lynx) to make sure your text is displayed properly. This is becoming more important with the use of cell phones and Personal Digital Assistants, like Palm Pilot, that surf the Web in text-only format. You may have to design your site specifically for the text device you are targeting.

23. When appropriate, provide some entertain-
     ment value to your visitors. This increases
     the time visitors stay on your site.

24. Develop your site with a standard screen
     resolution of 800x600. The majority of Web
     users have their computer monitors set to
     this resolution or higher.

25. Program your site to automatically change
     graphics and/or content each time a viewer
     visits your site. This makes your site appear
     fresh and dynamic. For example, if your site
     content uses quotes or facts, develop an
     automatic generator that allows visitors to
     read a new quote or fact when they first log
     into your site.

26. You can make your pages look like they
     have more graphics than they really do by a)
     putting an eye-catching logo at the top of
     each page, b) using a colored bullet to set off
     key points in the text, and c) using colored
     boxes and text that load instantly. But don't
     go overboard on bullets and colors. Always
     use them for a purpose, not just because
     they look "cool."

27. Limit your use of unique text colors because the browser may not translate the color properly. This could make reading your information difficult for the visitor.

28. As a general rule, for faster page loading, limit the size of all images used on a page to 50KB. If a picture or graphic is especially important, consider using a thumbnail-sized picture of the image and linking to the full-size copy (with a warning that the large graphic may take longer to view). If a thumbnail-sized picture looks terrible, consider cropping your image to make it smaller instead.

29. Build sites for version 4.0 of Netscape Navigator and Internet Explorer. Older versions are virtually extinct and later versions can read anything the 4.0 versions can read.

30. Make sure you test your site on multiple brands of browsers (especially Netscape Navigator/Communicator and Internet Explorer versions 4.0 and newer) and computer platforms (such as Windows and Mac

OS). One browser can portray your site perfectly, while another may display it improperly. By checking all major browsers and computer platforms, you will be assured everyone sees your site as you intended. This is a major issue with Web site design and should be an important consideration when building a site or selecting a company to build your site for you.

31. Optimize the load time of your site. Most people will only wait 10-15 seconds before moving on to another Web site. Consider that many people still use the slower 28.8KB modems to access the Internet. To appeal to both slow connections (28.8KB) and those visitors on fast broadband connections such as digital subscriber lines (DSL) or cable modems, consider having both a standard version of your Web site and a "souped-up" version for surfers with broadband access. Give visitors the option to click on either one from your home page. Although it requires extra development effort, you are not limited in your creativity and you will appeal to a larger segment of your target audience.

32. Don't use excessive animation. Providing entertainment is all right, but obnoxious blinking, spinning, jumping, etc. distracts the reader from the content.

33. To avoid confusion, use the standard color scheme for text hyperlinks on your site. The standard is blue for not yet visited links, and purple for already visited links.

34. Make sure your Web pages print out properly as many people print out Web sites to read them. Test the print function with different browsers and printers to make sure pages print the way you intended them to print.

35. Create Web page templates for individual product groups and business units within your organization. Rather than risk the chaos of each group creating its own pages, a template allows them to import their

information into your consistent, well-planned page style.

36. Limit the number of primary colors you use on your site to two or three. Using too many colors in your on-line identity may confuse potential visitors and you could lose any brand equity you could have gained from a cleaner looking site.

37. If you have registration forms on your site, and you are targeting international markets as well as the United States, make sure there is enough space for foreign addresses and codes. Many on-line forms set a 5-digit limit for zip codes, which instantly prevents people in most other countries from being able to enter accurate information.

38. To determine which site design and style works best for your audience, consider creating multiple test versions of a site and then place enough banners on search engines to draw significant traffic. Each user who clicks on an ad is linked to one version or another. Then analyze the site server logs to find out which version holds the visitor's attention longer and entices them to buy.

Content Is Critical

Content: the topics or matter treated in a written work; the amount of specified material contained.

Many experts agree that content is king on the Internet. The longer you can keep someone engaged on your site, the more opportunity you have to profit. If visitors do not find value in your site, they will not be motivated to return.

Here are a few tips to keep in mind when developing and adding your content.

39. Don't use acronyms without definitions. That's like reading a foreign language to the uninitiated visitor.

40. Speaking of foreign languages, remember that it's the World Wide Web. Consider a page with instructions in other languages. According to translation experts, English, French, German, Japanese and Spanish are the most used languages on the Internet.

41. Provide useful content on each page. Ask yourself "why should my target audience care about this page?" If you cannot legitimately answer this question, it probably does not provide value to your visitors and should be removed.

42.   Avoid strange humor. What's funny to you may not be so funny to your visitors. Be careful not to alienate your target audience who may not appreciate your humor.

43.   Always include an area for recruiting new talent to your organization. It's an inexpensive way to attract good people who may be interested in working for you based on your well-designed Web site.

44.   Be careful not to go overboard on text. Only 16% of Web users actually read word for word. As a general rule, write about half as many words for the Web as you would for a printed page. Writing in a format that is short and factual tends to work best. You can use the journalist technique: headline, sub-headline, and key information right at the top. If your visitors require a complete document for printing or saving, consider providing a separate link to it.

45. Content with spelling errors and typos reflect poorly on your company. Besides running your Web site content through a spell-check program, be sure to have others proofread it too.

46. Don't use video clips just to make your site look cool. People visit sites to get information and they want it as quickly as possible. Since video clips are slow to download, they

should be limited to situations where the information can't be conveyed with text or static images. Selling movies or devices that are hard to describe is a good example.

47. Make sure to answer the reader's WIIFM question (What's In It For Me) right at the beginning. If you don't give reasons why they should pay attention to your content—they won't.

48. Include newsletters and feature stories to personalize your site. Be sure to write them as a value-added resource for your visitors, not merely as a vehicle for advertising your site.

49. If your company has any press releases, information kits, or background articles, be sure to post them on-line in an easy to find list. If a reporter visits your site, you want to make it as simple as possible for him or her to find relevant information and give you free publicity.

50. As long as it's original, you can protect all the material on your Web site, including the written text and graphics by placing a copyright notice on your site in a prominent place.

51. When you include links to other Web sites, write complimentary text describing the link to help visitors understand what benefit they will get from the link. People don't like to waste time with useless resources, so help them understand what value they receive if they click on a particular link. If you are unsure of the value to your target audience, consider deleting the link.

52. Your site should have a legal page so visitors can see the rules for usage. It should also prohibit uploading and downloading materials on the site (especially those owned by third parties), and expressly prohibit the re-publication, reproduction, or distribution of any materials on the site without written permission.

53. If your site has a bulletin board or on-line forum, the legal page should also clearly state that offensive materials can and will be removed from the site at your sole discretion. In addition, the page should describe you as a "distributor" of information that does not approve nor disapprove of the opinions of others. Discourage the posting of names or other ways of positively identifying people

who post things on your site to maintain their privacy.

54. Provide a search feature for information within your Web site if it improves accessibility to content. Clearly state the scope of the collection topics being searched (e.g. your entire site or just certain portions of it).

55. A Web page can be designed to load text first from top to bottom. Consider giving visitors some fast-loading text near the top to read while waiting the (seemingly interminable) 15 seconds for the rest of the page and images to load. This will keep their attention, and they won't be as likely to get impatient with your site.

56. Using more than two typefaces makes a page look busy and may hamper your message. In fact, mixing several typefaces looks like you can't make up your mind.

57. It's never too early to create a FAQ page (Frequently Asked Questions) to address common problems and questions regarding your products and services. This allows customers to help themselves and reduces

the number of hours staff members spend dealing with customer concerns.

58. Consider creating different e-mail addresses to control feedback. Your operation will be more efficient if you can funnel order-status questions straight to customer service while shunting product inquiries directly to sales.

59. Try not to make the page longer than the window. Like a fold in a newspaper, the bottom edge of the browser window will stop some people from reading further. Keeping the content to the size of the browser window will allow readers to see what is presented at a glance.

60. Put a title header on each page, separate from the rest of the page's content. It doesn't need to be large or bold, as long as it's recognizable as a title. This will help orient the reader.

61. If a page is long with several distinct sections, consider a brief table of contents at the top of the page, with hyperlinks to each particular section. This allows readers to navigate more rapidly to the section they want.

62. If you have any information that is proprietary, don't post it on your Web site without any password protection. You are only encouraging someone to download, copy, and distribute that information without your permission.

63. Combining broad-based appeal topics (such as top news, financial information, or weather) with focused and unique content is a powerful way to attract and retain visitors. Consider what "up-to-the-minute" news sites you could link to or associate with that would compliment your own content.

64. Product-specific pages should be optimized for on-line reading, easy downloading, and printing by users. Printed pages should print on only one page if possible because formatting may become misaligned as the printer prints secondary pages.

65. The top of your page gets by far the most attention. However, if your site has an entrance page (sometimes called a splash page or doorway page) with only a logo and graphic that visitors see before your home

page, you take the chance that they will never see your product and service pages. Consider adding links to your most important pages on the entrance page to ensure that your most important products, services and pages are seen from the first moment the reader clicks to your site.

66. Personalize your content to build a better relationship with your visitors. Ways to personalize content include tailored e-mail alerts, account access, personal productivity

tools, wish lists, and product recommendations based on previous and/or intended purchases.

67. Every click is a burden for busy Web users, but more important, users don't like parting with their personal data before they have developed a sense of trust in the site. Therefore, postpone registration as far as possible into the usage process: if you ask too early before you have established your value to a new customer, you will simply turn away the prospect or they will enter bogus name and address information just to spite your system.

68. To write compelling content, use words and sentences that help messages be easily interpreted by the reader, such as with the use of examples, analogies, metaphors, symbols, stories, picture words, colloquialisms, etc. You can also repeat key messages by substituting certain words with synonyms and adding new pieces of information each time the message is repeated. You can also utilize more powerful words:

Don't Use	*Use*
Cost	Investment
Products/Services	Solutions
Cost-effective	Return on Investment
Inexpensive	Economical
But	And

TACTICAL TIPS

Tactical: small-scale actions serving a larger purpose; made or carried out with an immediate end in view.

While most companies can get a functioning Web site up and running, the ones that will have success are the ones that understand the tactical side of Internet marketing. Although the following list is not intended to be all-inclusive, it is still a good starting point. Don't forget to review the Advertising, Search Engine, and Community chapters in this book for additional tactical ideas.

69. If you're not asking for some kind of interaction from your visitors (such as information about their preferences, product feedback, or a new order), you're not using the medium to its fullest potential. Make your visitors feel comfortable about giving information to you. Get their permission first, let them know why you need the information, and explain how they can change the information later.

70. Establish an ironclad privacy policy for visitors who register on your site and NEVER rent or sell their names. Unless you are AOL, the value of your list to others is not worth jeopardizing your relationship with your site visitors. Many customers will not place a purchase if the Web site does not have their privacy policy clearly displayed. Things to include in your privacy policy include the following:

◇If you don't place cookies on your customer's computer (many big sites do), state it in your privacy policy.

◇If you don't have time to dote on each customer's statistics, say so in your privacy policy.

◇Be sure to tell customers about your secure ordering process. If you enter credit card orders by hand, put it in your policy.

◇Shoppers feel better when they know a real human is handling their order. Include a phone number where customers can reach you. Also include a regular mailing address (preferably a physical address, not a post office box).

71. Get permission to market to your registrants by asking them if they would like to be notified of special announcements generated by your company. Then continually adjust and customize the benefits you're providing to them to keep that permission going. This will build loyalty with your visitors.

72.   Skepticism is one of the greatest objections to
      overcome on the Web today. Visitors have
      heard of the scams on the Net, or may have
      been victims themselves. One way to resolve
      this is to join the Better Business Bureau
      Online and the TRUSTe organization. There's
      a fee involved, requirements you must meet,
      and standards you must agree to. However,
      it's well worth the credibility it brings to be

able to display their logo on your order forms and Web page. For more information: www.bbbonline.com and www.truste.org.

73. Always provide an incentive for the visitor to register and return at a later date. This can be new content, a contest, or something else of interest.

74. Give away services to lock the visitor in as a customer and tie them to other products (e.g., offering a reminder system for birthdays and anniversaries). In addition to prompting purchases directly, such services engender user loyalty.

75. Offer specials weekly and consider printable coupons from your site. Repeat customers will bring other new customers with them. Word of mouth referrals are one of the strongest forms of marketing you can utilize.

76. Offer a safe shopping guarantee. If visitors experience fraudulent credit card use on your transaction, offer to pay the $50 fee charged by the credit card company.

77. Offer an affiliate, commission-only program (if you sell products) to other sites that direct visitors to you. On your home page, publicize your offer to all site owners who may be interested in entering into a referral agreement with you.

78. If you participate in another company's affiliate program, you can boost your commissions by using the product yourself and then giving your readers a personally written recommendation. Your visitors will more likely be interested in purchasing the product if they believe in your endorsement.

79. When a visitor registers on your site or sends an e-mail suggestion, make sure they receive an automatic e-mail acknowledgment and thank you. Personalize the e-mail if possible by using a mail-merge program for the body of the text, or a customized programming script that adds the person's name to the subject line. Internet sites that provide more information about automatic e-mail acknowledgments include: www.sendthis.com, www.sendfree.com and www.zinfo.net.

80. Send regular e-mail to your customer data-
    base. Keep the messages short and address
    only one topic. Tailor them if possible,
    rather than sending a broadcast "blast" to
    the entire database.

81. For electronic prospecting, create a catchy e-mail subject line title to ensure the recipient will read it. Writing your subject line after you have written the text often makes it easier to come up with a compelling title. Keeping a file of all the e-mail you have sent will give you ideas for the future so you don't have to continuously write from scratch.

82. Consider "viral marketing" instead of bulk e-mail. Viral marketing is developing a game, puzzle, or funny entertainment that people will e-mail to their friends for a laugh. Recipients will read the e-mail because it is from someone they know. The messages have tremendous pass-along potential because they're fun. The sponsoring company gets their advertising message portrayed in a subtle or clever manner, and some can even be designed to track customer response. See Virtual Inventions at www.thevirge.com for more information.

83. In your e-mail program, create a "signature" to be placed at the bottom of all your e-mail correspondence. Include a link to your site (complete with "http://" to make it a live link to your site), as well as your

phone number. A good example of a signature is as follows:
Peter Alexander
WinWinWeb Internet Marketing
(925) 820-6155
http://www.winwinweb.com

84.   Form alliances with complementary companies and Web sites to improve your exposure and provide your visitors with other products and resources. To form the most effective alliances, try the following: a) select merchants who offer products/services that appeal to your audience, b) write product/service reviews and offer an easy link for your audience to purchase the product/service being reviewed, and c) offer your audience the option of submitting their own reviews of products/services they've used.

85.   Develop a niche Web site on a particular topic and "piggy-back" onto alliance companies and competitors' Web sites. You can save money on content development and gain a reputation as a one-stop shopping source for a wealth of related information on the Web.

86. Keep tabs on what your competition is doing (contests, activities, etc.) on the Web. Don't let them get a jump on your prospects just because you weren't paying attention. Sometimes, all you have to do is copy what they are doing (assuming it's successful) rather than reinventing the wheel.

87. Submit your new site or any new pages of your site to "cool sites of the day" (www.coolsiteoftheday.com) or other Web sites that have similar review sections. Many sites submitted receive a "star" or similar rating system, and if your site receives high praise, you can include this information in future promotional efforts. In

addition, Web sites that perform reviews may send out e-mail to their subscribers, announcing your site award. This drives more visitors to your site. For example, advertising's most respected award, the Clio, has an interactive category. To see previous award winners, check out the site at www.clioawards.com.

88. If you link to someone else's Web site, it's good etiquette to get their approval first. Some sites might not want the exposure that you are providing.

89. Anytime you have something newsworthy to announce, send out an electronic press release using one of the press release services listed in the Resources section of this book. To be most effective for a Web audience, the title of the announcement should include a key-word phrase that you want people to search on (e.g. "project management software") and it should be written simply so it fits on one page. Remember to include the contact information (domain name, telephone, e-mail) and send it out as text in your message, not as an attachment (editors are leery of opening attached files because of viruses).

90. Choose a product to serve as a loss leader (something you are willing to sell below its market value). Then list it on a popular auction site like eBay (www.ebay.com), along with a link that has a picture of the product on your Web site. This is a cost-effective means of bringing targeted traffic to your site. As long as your page provides

compelling content for the product listed on the auction site, you may generate several inquiries.

91. Make it easy for prospects and customers to respond the way they want to. Offer the opportunity to respond via e-mail, a toll-free number, a fax, or by mail. By providing all of these opportunities, you will appeal to a larger segment of your target audience.

92. Implement a wish list that allows shoppers to add items to their on-line wish list, which can be viewed by family and friends. This provides the opportunity to remarket to customers at a later date. After the holidays, you could e-mail a note to the customer letting them know that "unfortunately, nobody bought the gift you wanted, so here is a $20 gift certificate and free shipping if you want to buy it for yourself."

93. Utilize "pop-up" windows when a user's mouse hovers over a link or when the user visits or leaves a particular Web page. Use them to make free offers to your visitors, but not as a repeat of a banner ad. Do something

special, like highlight new products or services, contests, or back issues of newsletter, etc.

94. Install a feature like "Make Me Your Home Page" that allows a user to change the home page setting of their browser to your Web site at just the push of a button. Your Web site stays configured as their home page even if they close their browser or shut down their PC. And when your visitor logs on again, you're Web site will be the first thing they see each and every time. This is a great way to get repeat traffic, but make sure you have frequent, fresh content or else the surfer will eventually remove your site. See www.MakeMeYourHomePage.com.

95. Try to secure a toll-free telephone number that spells out the same name as your Web site address. Integrating your telephone and Web site name reinforces your branding efforts.

ADVERTISING CAN WORK

Advertising: the action of calling something to the attention of the public by paid announcements; emphasizing desirable qualities so as to arouse a desire to buy or patronize.

There are many different opinions on the power of advertising. Some people think it is unnecessary and raises the cost of the product. Others believe that advertising keeps the price down because the more people know about the product, the higher the sales volume.

In any case, there is no doubt that a well-executed advertising campaign will have an impact. In fact, when you get right down to it, most activity on the Internet can be considered a form of advertising in that you're trying to get your message in front of the people most likely to buy your products or services.

Listed below are a few Internet advertising tips to help increase your Web site's chances for success. These actions are by no means mandatory, but they definitely can make a difference.

96. Participate in banner exchange programs like www.smartclicks.com, www.linkexchange.com, www.webring.org or www.hyperbanner.net. In exchange for allowing

someone's banner on your site, you get to place your banner on their site. Although you're required to put someone else's banner on your site, it's an easy and cost-effective way for you to expand your presence on the Web and boost traffic to your site. To be most effective, limit your links to sites that are complementary to yours and cater to the same target audience.

97. The first quarter of every year is the best time to buy low-cost banner ads. Use them to build your name in the minds of prospects. Since January and February are traditionally cold months in the United States, many more people spend days and evenings indoors surfing the Web.

98. Use simple, distinctive designs for your ads. A good technique is to include a blue border around the banner to imply the whole banner is clickable. Bright color combinations (blue, green, and yellow for example) are also effective.

99. When designing a banner ad, wider is typically better (60 x 480 pixels is the widest standard). This improves the chances someone

will see it. However, keep the file small (10-15KB) to ensure it loads quickly. For standard banner sizing, go to the Internet Advertising Bureau's Web site: www.iab.net/iab_banner_standards/bannersource.html.

100. Place your banners on sites or pages most likely to be visited by your target audience. For example, if Golfers are your target audience, placing your banner on the home page of ESPN means you'll be paying for all sports enthusiasts to see your ad. But if you place your banner on the Golf page at ESPN, your cost will go down and you will be more likely reach your target audience.

101. Refresh banners often. Statistics show that the average banner ad "burns out" after two weeks or 200,000-400,000 impressions. One way to do this is by presenting a variety of messages in the same visual style.

102. Feature a Call to Action ("Click here for XYZ offer", "Free", etc.) or create urgency ("Last chance", etc.) on or below the banner to entice

the viewer. In addition, using questions
("Have you been to Hawaii lately?") are effective because they initiate interaction with the
potential customer. Keep in mind that if you
don't get them to respond as soon as they see
the ad, they probably won't respond at all.

103. Make sure that the page that the banner
points to is relevant to what the banner is
advertising. The page should give the visitor
options for different actions such as: "buy
now," "get more information," and/or "sign
up for our newsletter."

104. Animated banners are more noticeable, but
make sure they don't annoy the viewer or
take too long to load.

105. Position your banner ad at the top of the
page or somewhere in the immediately
viewable area of the Web page. If visitors
must scroll down to see your ad, they probably won't see it at all.

106. If your budget doesn't allow for fancy banner ads, consider using ads posted in on-line
newsletters and newsgroups. They are cheap
to produce and give you very inexpensive

ads. E-zines specialize in almost anything so they can reach a large targeted audience. See www.ezinesearch.com for a comprehensive list of on-line newsletters and magazines.

107. You might want to consider tracking your ads on the Internet. It's similar to placing a small ad in your local newspaper where you have people call your number and ask for extension "004." The extension number tells you where the person saw your ad. On the Internet, you would include an e-mail address like "info4@yourwebsite.com" or send shoppers to a Web address like "www.yourwebsite.com/publication4." The number four lets you know how many of your hits are coming from the ad you ran in publication 4.

108. One of the most effective forms of advertising is at the Point of Purchase (POP). The Internet has a great advantage in that everything can be POP. The customer sees a product, inputs their personal information, and purchases the product all within a short amount of time. Take advantage of POP by having your marketing messages throughout your Web site. For example,

include customer testimonials on your order form.

109. Whenever you run a new ad you need to continually monitor the performance of the ad to make sure your resources are well spent. Many Internet media and advertising companies provide monitoring systems as part of their service.

110. Consider rich text banner ads, which provide additional interactivity with the viewer (such as a game). Statistics show that these banners are one-third more likely to attract Internet surfers than standard banner ads. For more information about interactive rich text banner ads, review Engage's Web site at www.engage.com.

SEARCH ENGINE STRATEGIES

Search: to look into or over carefully or thoroughly in an effort to find or discover something; to uncover, find or come to know by inquiry or scrutiny.

Engine: something used to affect a purpose; a mechanical tool.

No Internet Marketing Tips book would be complete without a discussion of popular search engines. Popular search engines are often the #1 source for driving visitors to your Web site.

Since search engine technology changes so rapidly, it would be pointless to share programming tips because they will probably be outdated by the time you read this book. However, there are some basic rules to follow that are not easily dated.

111. Purchase a reputable tracking software package to analyze your site, such as WebTrends, or hire a company to do it for you. The more you know about who is visiting your site and how they got there, the better you will be prepared to increase your Internet presence.

112. If your tracking software suddenly indicates that a search engine stopped sending you multiple visitors, you may need to re-register with that engine. Many times the major search engines re-index themselves and drop off inactive or older Web sites.

113. Concentrate your efforts on getting listed on the major search engines. A good listing in a search engine that promotes itself and has strategic alliances is more likely to bring traffic than lesser-known search engines. They also have the resources to be well maintained and updated as the Web grows.

The major players in the search engine game include Alta Vista, AOL/Netscape, Excite, HotBot, Go, LookSmart, Lycos, Northern Light, Snap, WebCrawler and Yahoo! Also popular are the "meta" search engines such as Ask Jeeves, Find.com, or AllTheWeb.com. These search tools search multiple search engines at the same time to come up with better results than any one search engine.

114. Because Yahoo is so critical to search engine success, here are a few other tips for getting your Web site accepted by their system:

 ◆Yahoo likes link pages, so consider adding one to your site.

 ◆If you're trying to get a second domain listed for the same company, make sure you use different contact information and present it in a new and unique way in a different category. Don't link back and forth between the first domain and the second. Keep them totally separate. Once they're indexed, then you can go back and link them together with no problem.

 ◆If you have a regionally specific site, consider submitting it in that area. Regional submissions sometimes have an easier time getting in because editors don't have quite as many submissions. Also, submitting to a category that doesn't have too many entries may help you get in faster as well.

◆If your Web site is tied to a particular event or news to where time is of the essence, you may have an easier time getting in the index.

◆Yahoo is comprised of two different services. The primary service is a link directory compiled by real people who visit your site and decide if it is worthy to be on Yahoo. As a secondary service, Yahoo uses a regular search engine to find sites their staff can't cover. Yahoo uses the Google search function for this service, so make sure your site is registered with www.Google.com.

115. Each page on your site should have a unique title, consisting of about four or five words, that reflects the theme of that page. Title lines are used by search engines for indexing. They also appear as browser bookmark labels and show up when the page is printed.

116. Each page should also include a description line that clearly describes your site. Search engines use this line to describe your site. Note: The description line is hidden in the Web page and is not in plain view.

117. Web pages should have a list of five or ten "key" words or phrases that best describe the nature of your Web site. These words are used by search engines to help index your Web site. Note: These words are hidden in the Web page so it is not in plain view.

118. The first few sentences of your main page must sell your service. If the two or three line description that the search engine extracts from the top of your page, or the hidden

description tag, sounds dull or unexciting, prospective visitors to the site will scroll right past you in the Search Engine's listing. Make sure those first few lines are enticing so the reader will visit your site.

119. If you have a well-known brand, it's worth lobbying the major search engines for editorial links (which give preference to your brand name) to ensure users can find you. Review the home page of each major search engine to determine the proper lobbying channels.

120. Go to the major search engines, search for those terms under which you want to be found, and see what sites come up. Then go to those sites that are complementary to your business and negotiate links with them.

121. Updating the content of each page on a regular basis, even just slightly, may help your pages stay listed longer. The indexing system of the search engine will consider your site "refreshed."

122. Some keyword phrases are very often misspelled when typed into search engines. By

targeting misspelled searches, you might tap into a market that is overlooked by the competition and have your company come up high on the search engine rankings. Success with this technique rests in targeting keyword phrases that are often misspelled.

123. Search engines tend to discriminate against sites that do not have their own domain name. If you have a Web site on a free hosting service, then the discrimination is even worse. Save yourself a lot of headaches and get your own domain name! The $35/year investment pays for itself quickly. You can purchase a domain with your best keywords in it, separating each word with a hyphen. This will often improve your rankings for those keywords.

124. Link popularity helps engines to determine the relevancy of a site to a specific search term. It is now becoming a more important part of their formula for higher rankings. Be proactive and seek out sites that are willing to link to yours as a resource. With strong content, your site will be attractive to other complimentary sites and help you rank higher on the major search engines.

125. Search engine experts recommend optimizing for the "Ask Jeeves" search function by placing questions that customers frequently ask in the title of your page. For example, marketers hear "Where can I get the best price on televisions?" By properly positioning this question in your Web site, you increase the likelihood of getting a top position at Ask Jeeves or other question and answer search engines.

126. The best way to draw in visitors from other countries is to ensure your site is listed with International search engines and directories. Yahoo!, Excite, and AltaVista offer multiple versions of their search services based in different languages:

AltaVista:
www.altavista.com/av/content/av_network.html

Excite:
http://chinese.excite.com/
www.excite.fr/
www.excite.it/
www.excite.de/
http://se.excite.com/

Yahoo!
http://docs.yahoo.com/docs/info
/kbridge.html
http://chinese.yahoo.com/docs/info
/bridge.html
http://espanol.yahoo.com/
www.yahoo.dk/

MAINTENANCE ROOM

Maintenance: preserve from failure or decline; to keep in an existing state.

One of the most common mistakes Web site owners make is to disregard maintenance. Once the site is developed, little attention is given to ongoing upkeep. Reputable Internet development firms agree that the best rule of thumb is to budget the same amount of money for annual maintenance of your site as for the development of your site.

Why is maintenance so important? The single most important reason is image. You never get a second chance to make a first impression. If visitors see outdated events, products, or dead links on your site, their impression of your organization will be hindered. In addition, search engines are constantly re-indexing and dropping sites that have not been recently updated. Finally, as technology continues to evolve, you should always be making enhancements to your site to take advantage of the most appropriate technology. The Internet is dynamic; why should you remain static?

Listed below are a few maintenance tips to consider:

127. Keep the content fresh by regularly adding or changing things on your site. You want to entice your visitors to return at a later date and nothing is more effective than frequently having new material to share.

128. If you are providing links to other resources or sites, make sure those links are still active. Remove any "dead" links from your site.

129. Keep a backup of your site on another server. You never know if your primary machine will fail, and if you don't have a backup it will be that much longer before you regain your presence on the Web.

130. Have a suggestion box where visitors can provide improvement ideas for your site. This is one way to listen to your customers and make your site work easier for them.

131. If you have a high-volume e-commerce site, consider putting up servers on the East and West Coasts in order for each to service its respective half of the country and also provide continuous service in the event of a physical disaster, such as an earthquake or major storm.

PORTALS AND VIRTUAL COMMUNITIES

Portal: an entrance or means of entrance

Community: a body of persons of common and professional interests scattered through a larger society; a group of people with a common characteristic or interest.

Portals began as search engines to help users find information or Web sites. To entice visitors to stay longer, portals have now expanded their services with such things as customizable news, stock quotes, weather reports, and free e-mail.

More specialized portals, called "vertical portals", specialize in particular subjects directed at the consumer market, such as books or travel. Business-to-business application portals that concentrate on supply chain partnerships are also becoming more common.

Community sites are an excellent way to build up a loyal database of users. A couple of community examples include www.ivillage.com and www.geocities.com. However, the more commercial the site, the less likely the site will attract regular users because most community participants do not want to feel like they are being "sold" to. Yet, if implemented and managed correctly, a virtual community Web site can result in a loyal and dedicated audience that you can market to.

132. Effective portals offer resources specific and appropriate for all aspects of a vertical niche. Don't clutter your site with any links that do not directly relate your market

niche's marketing mix (product, place, promotion or distribution).

133. Effective portals provide a solution to all stakeholders associated with the vertical marketing niche. End users, suppliers, and partners all must find value from the content and resources available in your portal. If they do, your portal site will be bookmarked by users and they will return frequently.

134. Portals are fully empowered when they are seamlessly linked with critical systems internal to the organization such as legacy systems, ERP and customer databases.

135. Focus almost exclusively on the users. Determine who the target is and what they need from your community, then provide it.

136. Make your virtual community a safe and fun place to visit. Provide a way for visitors to introduce and network with each other. Offer a way for people to post their profiles on the site so they can interact with other "like minds."

137. Allow early adopters (users who register on the site when it first launches) to become premium members like frequent flyer programs. Let these early adopters become experts and show off their talents in the chat rooms or bulletin boards of your virtual community.

138. Continuously survey visitors and ask them for suggestions or what they would like to see changed. Get their approval for design changes and additions to the site.

139. As the community grows, segment visitors by demographic, geographic, individual, industry, or some other way. This will ensure that people continue to interact with others of similar interests. Explain the philosophy of growth to the users.

140. For chat rooms and bulletin boards, the Webmaster must aggressively edit and index information for future member needs. Offer keyword searching to help find topics of interest. Make sure the questions raised by newcomers are quickly answered.

141. Offer a directory of resources and suggested sites. Invite vendors of appropriate, complimentary goods and services to participate.

A FEW BASICS ON E-COMMERCE

Electronic (E-) Commerce: the exchange or buying and selling of commodities on a large scale involving transportation from place to place using the Internet as the central medium.

If you are considering a sophisticated e-commerce site, we recommend hiring a reputable company to develop it for you. However, if you are just experimenting with the idea, there are many sites (including some of the major search engines) that can easily and inexpensively set up a "virtual store" for you. The tips listed below are for those of you who are new to e-commerce and are testing the water.

142. Your customers will want to help themselves as much as possible, so make it easy for them to do business with you. Talk to your best customers, and ask them for suggestions on how to develop your e-commerce site to meet THEIR needs. They can tell you what works and what doesn't.

143. If you're adding e-commerce capability to your site, start planning the modifications that will be required to make e-commerce a reality (such as a storefront or on-line catalog). Not only will your Web site be changed, but you must also ensure that your back end operations (your distribution system, ordering system, etc.) are compatible with the e-commerce format. Don't offer e-commerce capability if your organization cannot support it. You will lose goodwill with your customers.

144. The quickest and most cost-effective way to start doing e-commerce is by subscribing to a virtual store service such as Yahoo! Store. For a monthly fee, you get a fully operational store that can accept credit cards and process orders. There are many other competing services available to choose from.

145. Protect sensitive data, such as credit card information, with SSL (Secure Socket Layer) encryption. SSL prevents eavesdroppers from observing the commerce transactions and passwords that your visitors use to purchase your products or to access your site. Be sure to emphasize that security measures are in place. Many visitors will not give sensitive information or perform transactions unless they are assured it is secure.

146. Instill confidence and credibility to your site by clearly stating your guarantee. Be sure to have a link to your guarantee from product information pages as well as from ordering pages.

147. Joining an affiliate program can be the easiest way to generate revenue from your Web site. Affiliate programs pay commissions for

anyone who clicks through from your site to the affiliate site and buys something. Choose affiliates who offer products or services your visitors would be interested in.

148. Avoid "Clicker Shock", which is when an on-line merchant hides shipping and handling charges until the final stage of the transaction. This is especially true for commodities that are competing on price alone. Customers don't appreciate being lured by a low price only to be gouged by extra charges. At a minimum, provide an explanation of shipping charges on a link from the shopping page.

149. If you are going to accept credit cards, make sure your server can handle the transaction load. It's hard to predict the number of users that will be visiting your site at any given time. You can always run multiple computers with your Web site, but credit card transactions quickly become a bottleneck because they take 5-20 seconds each over the Internet. Larger merchants tend to perform their transactions off-line or on a separate transaction server. For the user, this is great performance improvement because he or she does not have to wait for the results to come

back. For the merchant it is good because a set of dedicated machines can perform commerce transactions.

RECOMMENDED READING LIST OF RESOURCES AND WEB SITES

Customers.Com: how to create a profitable business strategy for the Internet and beyond. Patricia B. Seybold. Times Business (Random House). Copyright 1998. A great resource for case studies on the application of Internet marketing and e-commerce.

Principles Of Internet Marketing. Ward Hanson. South-Western College Publishing. Copyright 2000.

An excellent overview on the subject of Internet marketing.

Electronic Commerce: A Managerial Perspective. Efraim Turban, Jae Lee, David King and H. Michael Chung. Prentice-Hall. Copyright 2000. If you need a single book on e-commerce, this one is a pretty good choice. It covers all the business issues related with establishing an e-commerce site.

Essential Business Tactics For The Net. Larry Chase. John Wiley & Sons, Inc. Copyright 1998. Simple case studies and tactics focused on the consumer marketplace.

Web Commerce: Building a Digital Business. Kate Maddox with Dana Blankenhorn. John Wiley & Sons, Inc. Copyright 1998. Good descriptions of key Internet marketing tactics such as personalization.

Marketing On The Internet. Judy Strauss and Raymond Frost. Prentice-Hall. Copyright 1999. Another simple to read book that has some relevant case studies other books have not considered.

Net Gain: Expanding Markets Through Virtual Communities. John Hagel III and Arthur G. Armstrong. Harvard Business School Press. Copyright

1997. A must have if you want to develop a virtual community.

The Internet Marketing Plan: A Practical Handbook For Creating, Implementing, and Assessing Your Online Presence. Kim M. Bayne. John Wiley & Sons, Inc. Copyright 1997. A how-to guide if you want to develop an Internet marketing plan yourself.

Useful Web Site Marketing Resources:

- ◆ www.internet.com/sections/marketing.html and www.wilsonnweb.com are good, general Internet marketing resource sites.

- ◆ www.personalization.com offers information about personalizing Web sites, and a company that provides personalization services is www.datasage.com.

- ◆ www.netb2b.com is Advertising Age's Net-Marketing Online. A business-to-business resource site for articles on e-commerce, promotion, design, ROI/measurement, 100 best B2B sites, and a list of reference developers.

- ◆ www.refdesk.com provides a reference site of the day, reference tools, encyclopedias, newspapers, facts pages with 2,000 sites, almanacs, search desk, thesaurus, dictionaries, city guides, and on and on.

◆ www.prgguide.com and www.wetfeet.com provide market research publications on various industries and companies.

◆ www.shipsmo.com is a site that does order fulfillment and warehousing of product for e-commerce vendors. Small and large companies can use the service.

◆ www.deepcanyon.com focuses on Internet marketing, Web and e-commerce research.

◆ www.glreach.com/globstats is a good resource for statistics on international users of the Internet.

◆ www.engage.com is a company that provides profiling and segmenting of Internet audiences based on banner advertising

◆ www.likeminds.com/solutions/websell WebSell, by Like -Minds, offers personalized, real-time response to your on-line visitors.

◆ www.bnj.com is a company that provides Direct marketing support. They have an interactive software program that allows a responder to get their information customized on the Web site simply by entering their PIN number.

◆ www.yesmail.com recruits people and businesses that give their permission to receive promotional messages targeted to their unique interests. Over 5 million members.

◆ www.delivere.com provides information to its members via their "mathlogic" system. Members voluntarily provide their interests, hobbies and other personal information by visiting the site and entering sweepstakes. Then DeliverE matches its clients' outbound e-mail programs with its members' interests and provides its members with information and offers about products and services.

◆ www.mypoints.com offers free rewards on the Internet. Members earn points every time they are on the Internet engaging in a marketing and promotional activity. It's similar to frequent flyer programs, where points are earned by shopping, reading e-mail, filling out surveys, taking advantage of trial offers, reviewing Web sites and referring others to the Mypoints Web site. Points are redeemed at major retailers.

◈ http://ecominfocenter.com/infosources /websites/statistics.html is the home page of the eCommerce Information Center. It is a great site offering e-commerce statistics, analysis and market research. For example, do you need to get a handle on how many Internet users there are? How many Web sites are out there? The amount of business activity on the Web? This site provides the answers.

◈ http://ecomresourcecenter.com is the home page of the eCom Resource Center. It offers numerous resources on e-commerce—specifically, it provides a basic look at how to plan, build, manage and promote an e-commerce-enabled Web presence.

◈ www.useit.com is by Jakob Nielsen, one of the Internet's experts on Web usability. It's a plain site but packed with very "usable" tips and information.

◆ www.ecommercetimes.com is where you can find out what's happening in the world of e-commerce and on-line business. Subscribe to their free weekly e-zine because it's always filled with the latest trends, news, interviews and issues that affect this dynamic environment.

◆ http://ecommerce.internet.com is the eCommerce Guide, part of Internet.com's growing library of up-to-date Internet information. While http://Internet.com is itself a must-bookmark, the guide provides everything you need and want to know about e-commerce, with a special section on marketing at http://internet.com/sections /marketing.html.

◆ http://cism.bus.utexas.edu is the home page of the Center for Research in Electronic Commerce. It is an info-packed site on e-commerce news, publications, links and resources. It was put together by the people at the University of Texas at Austin, which is a leading research institution in electronic commerce.

◆ www.anacom.com/articles/ is where Rep-
resentatives from Anacom (a transaction
processing company) have written and
reproduced a number of white papers about
doing business on the Internet, entitled "The
ABC's of eCommerce."

◆ http://sellitontheweb.com/ is where you
can get information, resources and answers
to questions like: Do you need a merchant
account? Are you looking for a good Web
host? In the market for a fulfillment company? eCommerce 101 offers tons of information for selling successfully on the Web.

◆ http://e-comm.webopedia.com is where
you can find out what terms like SSL, SET,
VPN or ERP mean. Visit the eCommerce Web
Encyclopedia (or "Webopedia") to find out
about e-commerce-specific terminologies,
phrases, expressions, acronyms and words,
from digital wallets to clicks-and-mortar.

◆ www.techweb.com has an e-business section,
called "Planet IT," packed with specific information, articles and statistics on electronic
business.

◆   www.ecommerceadvisor.com gives e-business webmasters the do's and don'ts of on-
line business and e-commerce.

◆   www.e-land.com is a good place for Internet
and e-commerce stats. For the most comprehensive research information on e-commerce,
as well as the latest news in the online world,
eLand is it.

◆   www.adbusters.org/main/index.html has a
satirical look at online advertising.

SUGGESTION BOX

If you have a tip or suggestion for future volumes of this book, we would like to hear from you. If we include your suggestion, we will give you free press and publicity by citing the source of the tip. All you have to do is e-mail us at info@winwinweb.com or fill out the form below, and then fax or snail-mail it to us at the following address:

WinWinWeb Internet Marketing & Strategy
Attn: Internet Tips Book
442 Diablo Road, # 122
Danville, California 94526
(925) 820-6155
Fax: (603) 687-3218

INTERNET MARKETING TIP SUGGESTION

Name:_____

Company:_____

E-mail Address:_____

Phone Number: _____

Suggestion/Tip:_____

_____

_____

_____

_____

I authorize WinWinWeb to include my Internet marketing tip in future editions of *"Internet Marketing Tips for Busy Executives."*

Signed: _____

Date: _____

Latest Updates

Since the Internet is a dynamic and ever-changing medium, we have established a Web page for updates and valuable additional tips to make sure your copy remains current until the next edition of this book is published. Please visit www.WinWinWeb.com/BookUpdates.html to review the latest updates.

ABOUT THE AUTHORS

Peter Alexander

 Peter has been involved with Internet Marketing since 1995 when he worked as the Marketing Director for a software start-up company in Silicon Valley. In addition, he has held various marketing and sales management positions in retail, transportation, human resources, and medical products. During the 1980's, he earned his BS and MBA degrees in Marketing Management from the California State University system.

In addition to this book, he has contributed to several articles in national publications including Technology Business, InformationWeek, Marketing News and Human Resources Executive. Peter also serves as a marketing instructor for the University Of California, Berkeley Extension where he developed an on-line e-commerce course titled "Marketing For E-Commerce."

John Nobrega

 John Nobrega has been designing and managing Web sites since Mosaic, the first Web browser, was introduced. He founded and now runs Raydiate, a successful Web and E-commerce company that provides Web site solutions for companies ranging in size from start-up to Fortune 500.

Previously, John was the Operations Manager and part-owner of a Silicon Valley start-up company that conducted e-commerce transactions over the Internet.

John earned a BA in English from University of California at Davis.